भूरे भालू, भूरे भालू, तुम क्या देख रहे?

Brown Bear, Brown Bear, What Do You See?

Pictures by Eric Carle

भूरे भालू, भूरे भालू, तुम क्या देख रहे?

Brown Bear, Brown Bear, What Do You See?

by Bill Martin, Jr.

Hindi translation by Awadhesh Misra

Mantra Lingua

भूरे भालू, भूरे भालू,
तुम क्या देख रहे?

Brown bear, brown bear,
what do you see?

मुझे एक लाल चिड़िया
देख रही।

I see a red bird
looking at me.

लाल चिड़िया,
लाल चिड़िया,
तुम क्या देख रही?

Red bird, red bird,
what do you see?

मुझे एक पीली बतख
देख रही।

I see a yellow duck
looking at me.

पीली बतख, पीली बतख,
तुम क्या देख रही?

Yellow duck, yellow duck,
what do you see?

मुझे एक नीला घोड़ा
देख रहा।

I see a blue horse
looking at me.

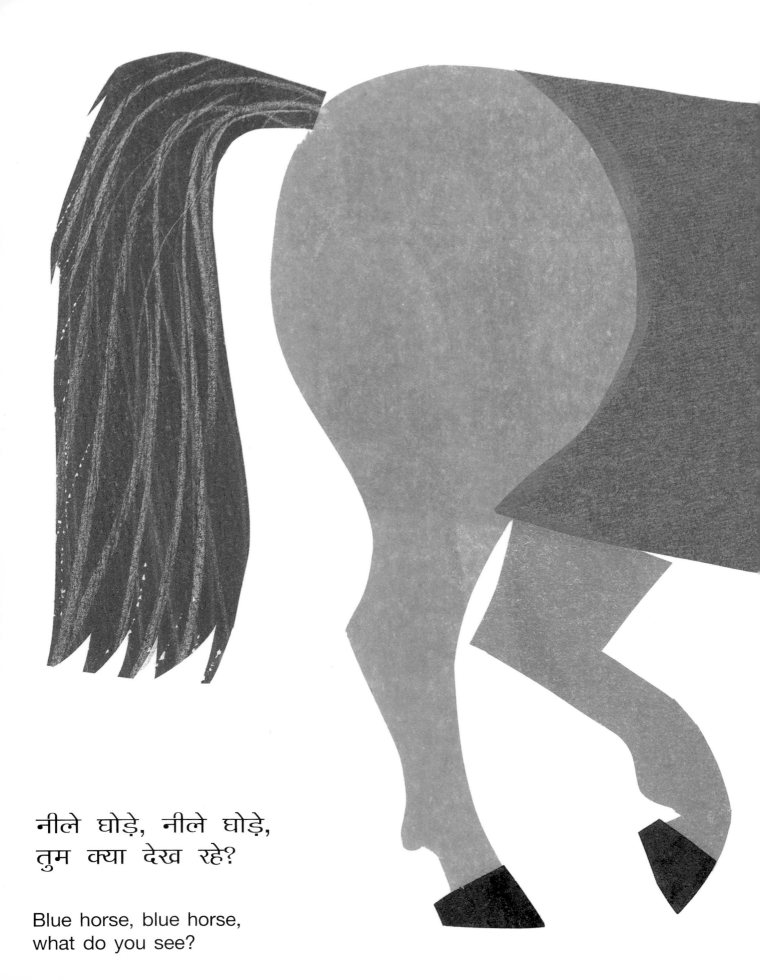

नीले घोड़े, नीले घोड़े,
तुम क्या देख रहे?

Blue horse, blue horse,
what do you see?

मुझे एक हरा मेंढक
देख रहा।

I see a green frog
looking at me.

हरे मेंढ़क, हरे मेंढ़क,
तुम क्या देख रहे?

Green frog, green frog,
what do you see?

मुझे एक
बैंगनी बिल्ली देख रही।

I see a purple cat
looking at me.

बैंगनी बिल्ली, बैंगनी बिल्ली,
तुम क्या देख रही?

Purple cat, purple cat,
what do you see?

मुझे एक सफेद कुत्ता
देख रहा।

I see a white dog
looking at me.

सफेद कुत्ते, सफेद कुत्ते,
तुम क्या देख रहे?

White dog, white dog,
what do you see?

I see a black sheep
looking at me.

मुझे एक काली भेड़
देख रही।

काली भेड़, काली भेड़,
तुम क्या देख रही?

Black sheep, black sheep,
what do you see?

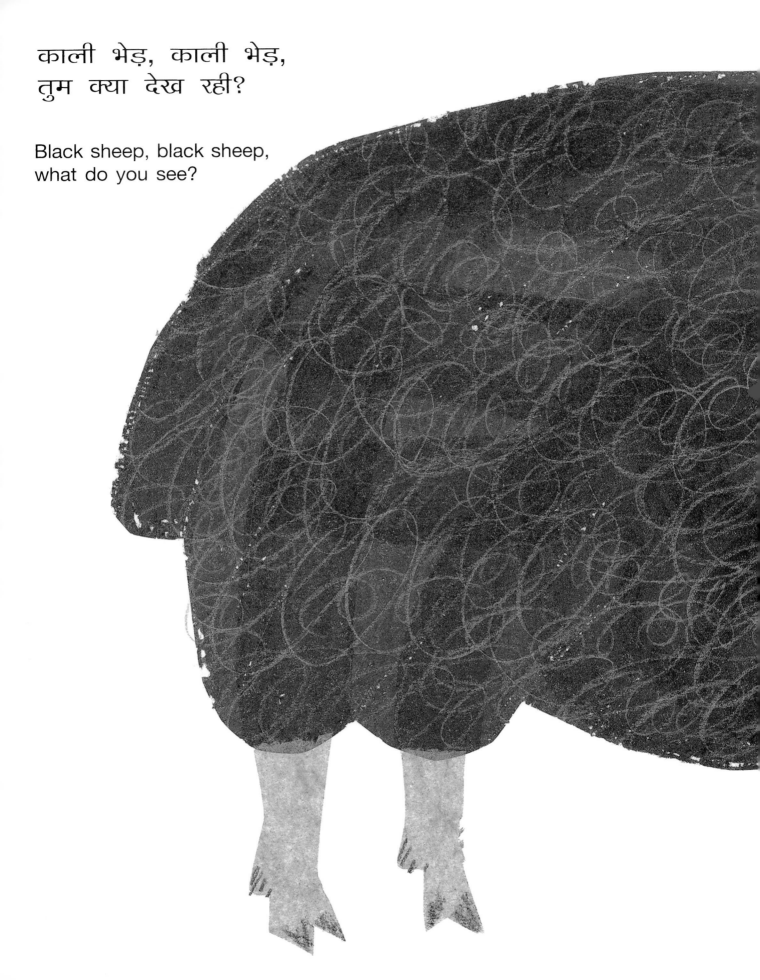

मुझे एक सुनहरी
मछली देख रही।

I see a goldfish
looking at me.

सुनहरी मछली, सुनहरी मछली,
तुम क्या देख रही?

Goldfish, goldfish,
    what do you see?

मुझे एक बन्दर
देख रहा।

I see a monkey
looking at me.

बन्दर, बन्दर,
तुम क्या देख रहे?

Monkey, monkey,
what do you see?

मुझे बच्चे
देख रहे।

I see children
looking at me.

बच्चे, बच्चे,
तुम क्या देख रहे?

Children, children,
what do you see?

एक लाल चिड़िया   a red bird

हम एक भूरे भालू को देख रहे हैं

We see a brown bear

एक हरा मेंढ़क   a green frog

एक काली भेड़   a black sheep

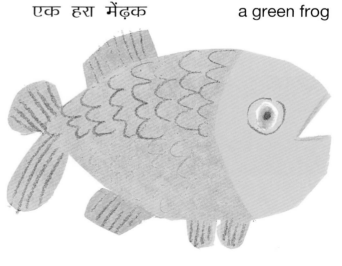

एक सुनहरी मछली   a goldfish

एक पीली बतख

a yellow duck

एक नीला घोड़ा

a blue horse

एक बैंगनी बिल्ली

a purple cat

एक सफेद कुत्ता

a white dog

और हमें एक बन्दर देख रहा।
हम यही सब देख रहे।

and a monkey looking at us.
That's what we see.

Text copyright © 1967, 1983 Holt Rinehart and Winston
Illustration copyright © 1984 Eric Carle
Dual language copyright © 2004 Mantra Lingua

This edition 2012

ISBN 978 1 84444 122 8

A CIP record for this book is available from the British Library

First published in dual language in Great Britain 2004 by Mantra Lingua Ltd
Global House, 303 Ballards Lane, London N12 8NP, UK
www.mantralingua.com

Printed in Hatfield,UK FP160812PB09121228